英語訳付き

ゆかたの着つけ ハンドブック

基本からお手入れまで ふだんづかいの楽しみ方

安田多賀子 著

A Casual Light-weight Yet Beautiful Type Kimono

THE YUKATA HANDBOOK

How to Wear and Care
for Japanese Traditional Summer Attire

Yasuda Takako

はじめに

　最初に思い浮かぶゆかたの思い出は、小学校三年生のときのことです。

　終戦を迎えた当時の日本にはまだ娯楽もなく、夏の楽しみといえば、盆踊りや野外映画会、そして長良川での花火でした。小学生の私は、母が仕度してくれた肩あげ、腰あげ、付紐のついたゆかたを自分で着て、兵児帯を結んでもらって、友だちと意気揚々と出かけたものでした。舗装のされていない砂利道を歩くので、下駄ばきの足はいつも泥だらけ。ゆかたを着た日は、足を洗い下駄を洗って干すことが子どもながらに習慣になっていたことを懐かしく思い出します。

　あれから60年以上経った今も、ゆかたは愛されつづけています。とくに最近では若い人に夏のファッションのひとつとして親しまれています。しかし、ゆかたを自分で着ることや、夏の日常着としての生活文化や知恵という日本人の感性の息づく部分は、「便利」や「楽」に取って代わられ、消えつつあるように感じています。

　本書では、今こそ身につけたいゆかたの基礎をお伝えしたいと思います。自分で着られることの楽しさが多くの人に伝わること、ゆかたが永遠に愛され着継がれることを願いつつ。

　　　　　　　　　　　　　　　安田多賀子

Introduction

My earliest memory of wearing yukata is when I was nine years old.

The Second World War had just ended, and there were not many fun things to do. In summer there was only the Obon dances, films shown out of doors and fireworks on the Nagara River. My mother took a yukata, put in tucks in the shoulders and hips and then attached a sash so it would fit a child. She tied a heko obi around me and I was ready. My friends and I were so excited to be going out! The roads were unpaved gravel and my feet were always getting muddy in my geta clogs. Rinsing off my feet and washing and hanging up my geta to dry after I wore a yukata remains a sweet memory for me.

More than sixty years have passed since then, but people still love to wear yukata. Nowadays young people are familiar with yukata as a summer fashion. But I think that a growing preference for convenience and ease means that putting on a yukata by yourself is a disappearing skill.

In this book I want to pass on the basic knowledge about yukata I want everyone nowadays to be familiar with. I hope that many people will discover the pleasure of putting on yukata by themselves and that yukata will continue to be loved and worn forever.

Takako Yasuda

協力／紫織庵

目次

CONTENTS

ゆかたの歴史
History of the Yukata

庶民が愛したゆかた

　ゆかたの起源は奈良時代、貴族が蒸し風呂に入るときに、水蒸気の熱さから身を守るために着用した「湯帷子」に始まります。「ゆかた」とは「湯帷子」の略です。

　江戸時代になると、綿栽培が盛んになり、庶民でも木綿を着られるようになりました。同時に銭湯が普及し、湯上がりにゆかたを着る習慣が広がっていきました。

　ゆかたを夏の街着として着用する習慣が一気に広がったのは、明治14年（1881年）、「古代形新染浴衣」というゆかたを題材にした歌舞伎が演じられたのがきっかけといわれています。また、染色の技術も進化し、それまでは藍染だと1日5反が精一杯だった染めが、「注染」という技法で、1日に何百反も染めることが可能になりました。さまざまな柄が数多く出回るようになり、それらをおしゃれに粋に着こなして、縁日や花火見物など、夏の夜の遊びを楽しむようになったのです。

Loved by the Common People

The origins of the yukata lie in the Nara period when the aristocracy wore a "yukatabira (hot water kimono)" in the steam baths to protect their skin from the heat. "Yukata" is short for "yukatabira".

In the Edo period, with the rise of cotton production, even commoners could afford to wear cotton. Public baths were becoming popular, and people started to wear a yukata after taking a bath.

Wearing yukata as summer street wear became widespread in 1881, following the popularity of a kabuki play that featured the yukata — "Kodaigata Shinzome Yukata". At the same time new dyeing techniques were being developed. For example, in the past only five bolts of cloth could be dyed with indigo in one day, but a new technique, chūsen dyeing, made it possible to dye hundreds of bolts in one day. Many new patterns became available, and dressing up stylishly on a summer evening to go to a festival or fireworks display became a popular amusement.

協力／紫織庵

7

ゆかたの特徴
What's Special About the Yukata

ゆかたはエコロジー

　ゆかたはエコロジーだといわれます。そういわれるのは、天然素材の木綿が使われていることがひとつ。また、外気を取り入れたいときはゆったりと着こなし、体温を保持したいときには衿元を深めにするなど、自然と調和した調整ができるのもその理由のひとつです。さらに、昔の人は、ゆかたをリメイク、リフォームしながら繰り返し着て、最後にはおしめや雑巾にまで利用していたそうです。このように長く活用できるところが、ゆかたがエコロジーといわれる所以でもあります。最近はそこまでしないかもしれませんが、ていねいに手入れをしながら長く着る──現代のゆかたのエコロジーはそこにあるのかもしれません。

The Yukata is Eco Fashion

The yukata is eco fashion. One reason is that it is made from the natural fiber cotton. Another reason is that how it is worn can be adjusted in harmony with nature: loosely when you want the air to flow through or tightly overlapped at the collar to keep your body heat in. In the old days people would remake and reform their yukata to wear over and over, and in the end use the material for diapers or cleaning rags. Being able to use the yukata for such a long time is another reason it is called eco fashion. People today may not go quite as far, but with proper care a yukata can be worn for a long time. Perhaps that is how the modern yukata is eco fashion.

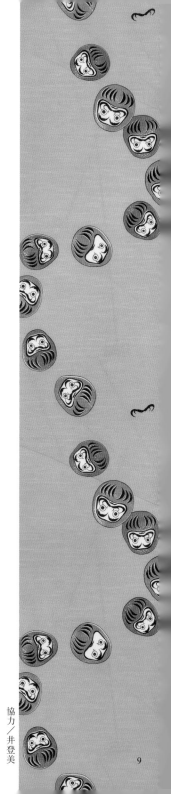

協力／井登美

9

ゆかたの特徴
What's Special About the Yukata

美しいゆかた姿の鍵

　夏のゆかた姿の美しさは、見た目の「涼感」によって決まります。涼しげかつさわやかな着つけとは、「きちんと」「きれいに」着つけることでもあります。これは窮屈だったり苦しかったりするものではなく、ポイントさえ押さえれば、ふわりと体にまとうことができ、着ていることが楽な着方です。着ている自分も涼やかで気持ちのいい着つけこそが美しい着姿の鍵なのです。

　また、きちんと仕立てられたゆかたを着ることも美しさの鍵です。自分に合わせて仕立てたゆかたは、顔映りのよい生地、その人に合った袖の丈や丸み、衣紋の抜き加減、柄の配置など、あつらえならではの技術が施されています。多少高額にもなりますが、美しい着姿に加え、質がよく長く愛用できるので、結果、賢い買い物といえるでしょう。

The Key to a Beautiful Look

When you look cool and comfortable in a summer yukata, you look beautiful. A graceful clean line is a cool, fresh look. This is not a matter of being stiff and tight — if you know the key points you can wrap yourself gently in a yukata and wear it comfortably. When you wear yukata so that you are cool and comfortable that is the key to a beautiful look.

Wearing a properly made yukata is also key to wearing it beautifully. A yukata that is made for you, in a fabric that flatters your complexion, with everything fitting you — the sleeve length and shape, the space at the nape of the neck, the placement of the pattern — is something only custom tailoring can provide. It may cost a little more, but it's a wise investment that pays off not only in a beautiful look but also in the high quality that you will love to wear for a long time.

協力／井登美

ゆかたの名称

Parts of the Yukata

前
Front

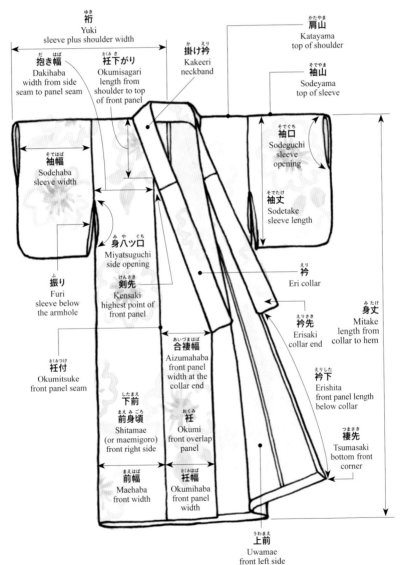

ゆき
裄
Yuki
sleeve plus shoulder width

かたやま
肩山
Katayama
top of shoulder

だきはば
抱き幅
Dakihaba
width from side
seam to panel seam

おくみさがり
衽下がり
Okumisagari
length from
shoulder to top
of front panel

かけえり
掛け衿
Kakeeri
neckband

そでやま
袖山
Sodeyama
top of sleeve

そではば
袖幅
Sodehaba
sleeve width

そでぐち
袖口
Sodeguchi
sleeve
opening

そでたけ
袖丈
Sodetake
sleeve length

みやつぐち
身八ツ口
Miyatsuguchi
side opening

ふり
振り
Furi
sleeve below
the armhole

けんさき
剣先
Kensaki
highest point of
front panel

えり
衿
Eri collar

みたけ
身丈
Mitake
length from
collar to hem

えりさき
衿先
Erisaki
collar end

おくみつけ
衽付
Okumitsuke
front panel seam

あいづまはば
合褄幅
Aizumahaba
front panel
width at the
collar end

えりした
衿下
Erishita
front panel length
below collar

したまえ
下前
まえみごろ
前身頃
Shitamae
(or maemigoro)
front right side

おくみ
衽
Okumi
front overlap
panel

つまさき
褄先
Tsumasaki
bottom front
corner

まえはば
前幅
Maehaba
front width

おくみはば
衽幅
Okumihaba
front panel
width

うわまえ
上前
Uwamae
front left side

12

ゆかたの各部にはきもの特有の名前がついています。着つけをするとき、あつらえるときに覚えておくと便利です。

The terms used are used for kimono. These names are useful to know when dressing or when ordering a new yukata.

後ろ
Back

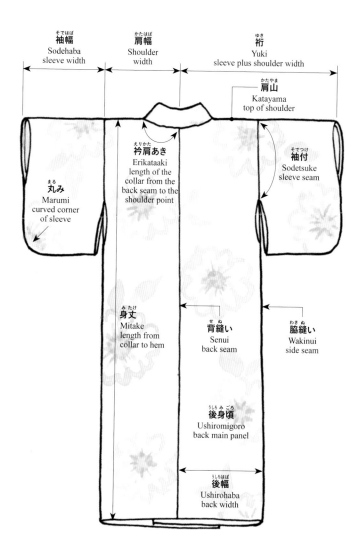

そではば
袖幅
Sodehaba
sleeve width

かたはば
肩幅
Shoulder
width

ゆき
裄
Yuki
sleeve plus shoulder width

かたやま
肩山
Katayama
top of shoulder

えりかた
衿肩あき
Erikataaki
length of the
collar from the
back seam to the
shoulder point

そでつけ
袖付
Sodetsuke
sleeve seam

まる
丸み
Marumi
curved corner
of sleeve

みたけ
身丈
Mitake
length from
collar to hem

せ ぬ
背縫い
Senui
back seam

わき ぬ
脇縫い
Wakinui
side seam

うしろ み ごろ
後身頃
Ushiromigoro
back main panel

うしろはば
後幅
Ushirohaba
back width

13

協力／紫織庵

きちんときれいに、ゆかたを着る
ゆかたの着方

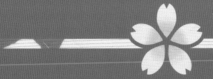

WITH A GRACEFUL, CLEAN LINE
WEARING
YUKATA

準備するもの

What You Need for Wearing a Yukata

上半身は綿や麻などの自然素材、下半身はスカートの裏地のようにサラリとしたものを選びましょう。

A natural fabric such as cotton or linen on top and a silky fabric on bottom are a good choice.

肌襦袢
はだじゅばん

Hadajuban underwear top

肌に直接着るものなので、通気性・吸湿性・速乾性に富んだものにしましょう。写真は綿麻楊柳素材です。

Something breathable, absorbent and fast drying is most comfortable next to your skin. The photo shows cotton-linen crepe.

ワンピースタイプの肌襦袢

One-piece underwear

初心者でも着やすいワンピースタイプ。肌色にすると透けないので安心です。

Simple for beginners. Skin color lingerie doesn't show under a light color yukata.

肌着
Underwear

16

着つけをする前にしっかりと準備をしましょう。ゆかたはきものと共通で使えるものがほとんどです。一式持っていると便利です。

Be sure to have everything you need on hand. You can use these when wearing a formal kimono, too.

ステテコ
Suteteko
underwear bottom

夏は汗で足がベタつくことがあるので、ステテコが快適です。写真はクレープ素材。ペチコートタイプのものでもよいでしょう。

Culottes are cool and comfortable in hot summer weather. The photo shows crepe. A half-slip type is also a good choice.

和装ブラジャー
Kimono bra

夏のきもの用を着用しましょう。バストのトップとアンダーの差をなくして、美しいなだらかなラインをつくってくれます。

Select a light summer type. The bra de-emphasizes the bust to create a classic Japanese body line.

ゆかたに衿をつけたい人
If you want to add a collar cover

はんじゅばん
半襦袢
Hanjuban underrobe

ゆかたに衿をつけて楽しみたい人は、半襦袢か長襦袢を用意してください。

Select a hanjuban half-length robe or nagajuban full-length robe (see p.77).

腰紐
Koshihimo sash

初心者は腰紐用と胸紐用に最低2本は必要です。帯をお太鼓結びにする場合は仮紐としても使います。

Beginners need at least two, one for below the waist and one for above the waist. You can also use one as a temporary tie if you will be tying your obi in a taiko knot.

伊達締め
Datejime belt

胸紐を締めたあとに締めます。胸元がくずれにくくなります。

Tied after the above-the-waist sash in order to keep the front of the yukata neatly in place.

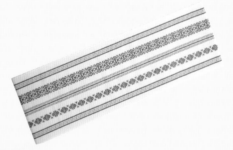

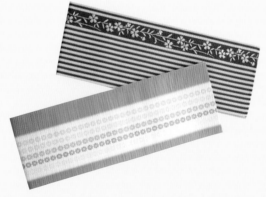

ゆかたのときは、あまり厚みのない
帯枕を使います。帯揚げは帯枕に
かけて使います（p76も参照）。

A flatter cushion is better with yukata.
Cover it with an obiage cloth (see
p.76).

帯揚げ
<ruby>帯<rt>おび</rt></ruby><ruby>揚<rt>あ</rt></ruby>げ
Obiage cloth

<ruby>帯<rt>おび</rt></ruby><ruby>枕<rt>まくら</rt></ruby>
帯枕
Obimakura cushion

<ruby>帯<rt>おび</rt></ruby><ruby>板<rt>いた</rt></ruby>
帯板
Obiita
stiffener

巻いたあとに帯の間に差しこむ
タイプ（a）と、帯を巻く前につけ
るゴムベルトがついたタイプ（b）
があります。

There are two types: (a) one
inserted into the obi afterward
and (b) one attached to an elastic
belt that goes on before the obi.

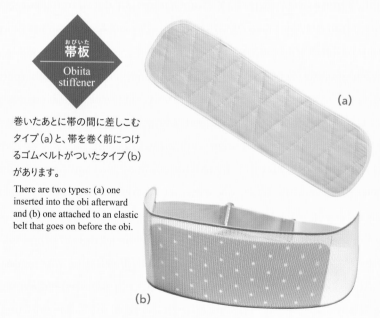

(a)

(b)

商品協力／井登美

ゆかたの着つけ
「きちんと」「きれいに」のコツ

Wearing Yukata — tips and pointers for a graceful, clean line

▸ How To

1

羽織ります。

Put the yukata on.

2

袖山

両手で袖山を持ち、両手を床に対して平行にのばします。

Hold one sleeve cap in each hand and hold your arms out straight.

> **POINT**
>
> 背中心を合わせる。
> Make sure the center is straight down your back.

3

衿の縫い目 Collar seam

左右のかけ衿の縫い目を合わせ、両衿を片手で持ち、もう片方の手で背縫いを持ちます。

Match the collar seams together and hold in one hand. Hold the back seam with the other hand.

◀ 背縫い Back seam

20

ゆかたを着るのであれば、「きちんと」「きれいに」着たいものです。受ける印象も、着心地もぐんと違ってきます。

You want to look well-groomed and elegant in your yukata. That makes the difference in the impression you make on others and how you feel wearing it.

4

POINT

衿抜きが美しいとゆかた姿もきれい。

The space at the nape is the key to a beautiful line.

背縫いを垂直方向に下に向かって引きながら、衿をこぶしひとつ分空けます。

Pull the back seam down straight so that the space between your neck and the collar is about the width of a fist.

5

両手で衿先から20cmぐらい上を持ち、ゆかたをヒップに沿わせるように前に引きます。裾線はくるぶしが隠れるぐらいに。

Use both hands to hold the collar about 20 cm above the ends and pull it forward around your hips. The skirt should just cover your ankles.

衿先 the end of collar

6

POINT

前裾をすこし斜めに上げる。

The bottom inside edge of the skirt angles up slightly(∗).

上前

すこし上げる(∗)

衿先が腰骨の位置にくるように上前幅を決めます。

Bring the left side over so that the end of the collar is at your hip bone.

▸ **How To**

⑦

すこし上げる(*)

下前

いったん上前を開いて下前を合わせて、下前の褄先をすこし上げます。

Unwrap the left side and bring the right side over. The bottom inside edge of the skirt angles up slightly(*).

8

上前を戻します。

Bring the left side over the right side.

9

上前を押さえながら右手を左に移動させ、左手で上前を上げながら、おなかのシワをしっかり伸ばします。

Hold the left side of the yukata firmly in place as you bring your right hand over to the left. Lift the left side of the yukata with your left hand and smooth out any folds around your waist.

POINT

おなか周りのシワはきちんと伸ばす。

Smooth out folds around the waist.

⑩

左手で腰紐を持ちます。

Hold the sash in your left hand.

⑪

合わせたゆかたがずれないように手で押さえながら、両手でウエストのやや下の位置に腰紐を当てて、締めます。

Hold the yukata firmly in place as you use both hands to center the sash slightly below your waistline.

⑫

POINT

腰紐の交差と、背中のシワ伸ばしを同時進行する。

Cross the sash in back and smooth out folds at the same time.

後ろで腰紐を交差させるときに、人差し指を腰紐の下から入れて、背中心からそれぞれ左と右にシワを伸ばしながら移動させます。

When you cross the sash in back, hook your index fingers under the sash from below to smooth out any folds to the left and right.

▸ How To

13

> **POINT**
> ここでしっかり締める。
> Keep it tight.

しっかり締めながら、腰紐を前に持ってきます。

Keep the sash tight as you bring it around to the front.

14

2回絡げて　Wrap around twice

締めて　Pull tight

逆に交差　Cross the other way

腰紐を締める。「2回絡げて、キュッと締めてから、逆に交差」は、緩まない、苦しくない紐結びなので覚えておきましょう。

Tie the sash in front. Wrap one end around the sash twice, pull tight, and cross the ends the other way. If you tie it this way, the knot won't come loose and it's still comfortable.

15

> **POINT**
> 腰紐の端は下から上に。
> Tuck up from below.

交差させた腰紐は、両側とも、巻いてある腰紐の下から上にはさみこみます。

Tuck the ends of the sash up under the sash from below.

16

おはしょり

この開きが
身八ツ口

手の甲を背中側にして身八ツ口から手を
入れ、中心から左右におはしょりの下のラ
インをきっちり伸ばします。

Put your hands inside from the miyatsuguchi
side openings with the back of your hands
against your back. Pull the bottom of the
ohashori fold at the back out smooth from the
center.

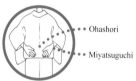

• • Ohashori

• Miyatsuguchi

17

この中で
下前の衿を
持っています

上前の衿 ←

前も同様に。最後に下前、上前の衿を持
ってピンと伸ばします。

Do the same for the ohashori fold at the front.
Then hold the left and right side collars and
pull them out flat.

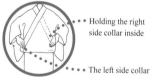

• Holding the right
side collar inside

• • • The left side collar

18

衿を整えてから、右手で下前の衿をたどり
ながら整えていきます。

Straighten out the top of the collar and then
use the right hand to straighten out the right
side collar.

▶ How To

下前の衿をたどって整えたら、
右脇に移動しておはしょりを持つ

この開きが身八ツ口

19

身八ツ口から左手で下前の衿を押さえ、
右手で下前のおはしょりの脇あたりを持ち
ます。

Put your left hand inside the side opening and
hold the right side collar in place. With your
right hand, hold the right hand side of the
ohashori fold.

• Miyatsuguchi

After straightening the right side
collar, bring your right hand over
to hold the right hand side of the
ohashori fold.

20

下前の
おはしょり

下前のおはしょりを持った右手と左手を
一緒に上に上げます。

Bring both hands holding the right side of the
ohashori fold up at the same time.

Right side ohashori fold

21

両手の平をクルリと回転させて、中のおは
しょりを三角形になるように、中に折りこみ
ます。

Roll your palms over each other to create a
triangular fold inside.

POINT

おなかあたりがスッキリ!
A flat, clean waist line!

22 右手で折ったおはしょりを、右から左へ整えます。

Use your right hand to smooth the fold from right to left.

23 右手で上前のおはしょりの下線を左から右へ整えます。

Use the right hand to straighten out the bottom of the left side ohashori fold from left to right.

Bottom of the ohashori fold

24 胸紐を前に当ててから後ろに回して交差させます。(12と同じ要領です)

Center the koshihimo sash at the center in front and cross in back (same as step 12).

▸ How To

25

キュッと締めます。13と同じ要領です。

Keep the sash tight (same as step 13).

26

紐を前に回して、14と同じ要領で結びます。

Bring the ends around front and tie the same way as in step 14.

POINT

2回絡げて、締めてから、逆に交差して結ぶ。

Wrap around twice, pull tight, and cross the other way.

27

交差させたあとの胸紐は左右とも、巻いてある胸紐の上から下にはさみこみます。

After crossing the ends the other way, tuck them down under the sash.

右袖がじゃまになるので、腕にクルリとか
け、身八ツ口を整える準備をします。

Wrap your right sleeve over your arm so it
won't be in the way. Now you're ready to
straighten out the side openings.

まずは後身頃をギュッと前に引っ張ります。

Pull the back of the yukata forward tightly.

つぎに前身頃を後ろにかぶせます。

Then pull the front of the yukata over the back.

▸ How To

31 最後に斜め前方に引っ張ります。反対側も同様に。

Then pull it forward down on the diagonal. Do the same on the other side.

32 伊達締めを締めていきます。まず、伊達締めをウエストの位置に当てます。

Now to tie the datejime belt. Position the sash at your waistline.

33 身八ツ口を押さえながら後ろに回し、背できれいに交差させます。

Hold the side openings closed as you wrap it around your back and neatly cross the ends.

右手側はまっすぐに、左手側は斜め上に
上げます。

The right-hand end is straight and the left-hand
end goes up on the diagonal.

左手側を写真のように折ります。

Fold the left-hand end as shown in the photo.

ここで1回キュッと締めます。

Pull it tight.

▸ How To

37

伊達締めを前に回して、14と同様に2回
絡げて、締めてから、逆に交差させて結び
ます。

Bring the belt around front. Wrap the end
around twice, pull tight, and cross the ends the
other way as in step 14.

38

交差させた両端は巻いた伊達締めにはさ
みこみます。上からでも下からでもかまい
ません。

Tuck the ends under the belt, from above or
below as you like.

> **POINT**
>
> 伊達締めがきちんとし
> ていれば、胸元がくず
> れません。
>
> The datejime belt
> keeps the front of the
> yukata neatly in place.

39

帯板をつけます。つぎはいよいよ帯を結び
ます。

Put on the obiita. Finally you're ready to tie
the obi.

協力／井登美

帯結びの基本
文庫結びの結び方
Bunko Knot — basic obi knot

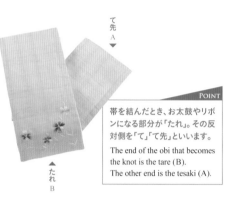

て先
A ▼

POINT

帯を結んだとき、お太鼓やリボンになる部分が「たれ」。その反対側を「て」「て先」といいます。

The end of the obi that becomes the knot is the tare (B).
The other end is the tesaki (A).

▲ たれ
B

ゆかたのときは一般的に半幅帯 (p40) で結びます。

A yukata is usually worn with an obi that is half the width of a standard kimono obi. This kind of obi is called a hanhaba obi (See p.40).

▸ **How To**

て先
A ▼

① て先を肩に預けて背中の腰ぐらいまでとり、巻きはじめます。

Drape A over your shoulder down your back to your hips and start to wrap the obi around your body.

② ふた巻きしたら、脇から三角になるように折り上げます。

After wrapping twice around, fold it up to make a triangle from your hips.

たれ B

こちらが輪
The fold is here

て先
A ▼

③ 肩に預けていたて先を半分の幅に折って右手で持ちます。

Take A from your shoulder and fold in half lengthwise. Hold it in your right hand.

34

文庫結びは、ゆかたではもっともポピュラーな帯の結び方です。結び方のポイントを押さえて、美しく仕上げましょう。

The bunko knot is the most popular knot for yukata. Learn the basic points so that you can tie a beautiful knot.

て先を下ろしながらたれとひと結びし、締めてから左肩にのせます。

Bring A down and tie once with B. Pull it tight and put it over your left shoulder.

POINT

しっかり広げることで、結び目が締まる。

Open it out fully for a flat knot.

下側のたれをしっかり広げます。

Spread out B.

肩幅の寸法をとって折り、残りも内側に折りこみます。

Fold a shoulder-width length (∗) and fold the remainder inside.

リボンの形になるように、中心でひだをとります。

To make the bow shape, pinch the middle together.

帯結びの基本　文庫結びの結び方

▸ How To

巻き込む
Wrap

て先 A

肩に預けていたて先を下ろして、リ
ボンの中心に下から巻きこみます。

Take A from your shoulder and wrap it
around the center of the bow from the
bottom.

て先 A

て先をしっかり上に上げます。

Bring A up tightly.

もうひと巻きして、胴回りの上線を
開きます。

Wrap around one more time. Open up
the two layers of the obi at the top.

て先 A

残りのて先を帯板と前帯のあいだ
に入れます。

Tuck the remainder of A between the
obiita and the obi in front.

⑫

・・・・下から引き出した
て先 A

て先を下から引き出して、羽の形
を整えます。

Pull A down from below. Shape the
sides of the bow.

⑬

右袖をp29の28のようにクルリと
腕にかけます。

Wrap your right sleeve around your
arm as in step 28 (p.29).

POINT

衿合わせに逆らわない
ように右方向に回す。

Turn to the right, the
same as the yukata
overlap.

⑭

POINT

て先を巻きこむことで帯
にシワが寄らず、リボン
がしっかり固定される。

Tucking in the rolled
up A keeps the bow
firmly in place and the
obi won't wrinkle.

て先は・・・・
出したまま
A is still
showing

右手で帯の上を、左手で帯の下を
持って、背中に回します。

Hold the top of the obi with your right
hand and the bottom with your left.
Turn the knot to the back.

⑮

このあたりまでもっていく
Up to about here

て先 A

羽を背中に回したら、下に出ている
て先をクルクルと帯の中央ぐらい
まで巻きこみます。

When the knot is in the back, roll up A
to the middle of the obi.

仕上げのチェック
美しいゆかた姿のポイント
Final Check Points for a Beautiful Look

仕上げのチェック　美しいゆかた姿のポイント

前の仕上がり
Front

POINT ②

前帯はふた巻きした
帯が斜めにずれてい
ると、粋な雰囲気に。
The doubled part of
the front obi slightly
out of line looks
stylish.

POINT ①

衿合わせはきっちりと!
Collars neatly
together.

POINT ③

帯の下線とおはしょり
は平行にします。
Bottom of the obi and
the ohashori fold are
even.

POINT ④

前裾上がりになって
いる。
Front of the skirt hem
is slightly higher than
the back.

最後に、きちんときれいに着つけられたかチェックしましょう。

Make a final check for a graceful, clean look.

後ろの仕上がり
Back

POINT 5

ゆかたの背縫いが背
中心に合っている。

Back seam centered
down the back.

POINT 8

帯にシワがよってい
ない。

No wrinkles in the
obi.

POINT 6

帯の上に余分なたる
みがない。

No extra fabric above
the obi.

POINT 7

リボン（羽）が帯の上
線の上にしっかりの
っている。

Bow sits securely on
top of the obi.

帯の種類
Types of Obi

　一枚のゆかたも、合わせる帯で印象が変わってきます。最初の一本は、綿か麻素材の半幅帯にすると便利です。素材は、締め具合のよさ、通気性のよさから、綿、麻、紗（絹）などの自然素材がおすすめです。帯には以下のような種類があります。特徴を知って、使って、あなたのゆかたライフに素敵なエッセンスを!

- **半幅帯**　一般的な帯の半分の幅で、およそ15〜17cmくらいです。
- **八寸帯**　おもに織物素材の帯で、お太鼓になる部分のみ二重に仕立てられています。
- **兵児帯**　芯の入っていない柔らかな帯。おもに男性や子ども用に使われます。
- **博多帯**　独特な模様で絹が一般的。江戸時代、黒田藩から幕府への献上品でした。
- **六寸帯**　半幅帯と八寸帯の中間の幅。背の高い人におすすめです。

With a different obi the same yukata can make a completely different impression. A cotton or linen hanhaba ("half width") obi is a good choice for your first obi. Natural fibers such as cotton, linen and silk gauze are breathable and wrap well. Here are some different types of obi. Get to know their special characteristics and use them to make your yukata even lovelier!

- Hanhaba obi Half the width of a standard obi, or about 15 to 17 cm wide.
- Hassun obi Usually woven fabric, with only the outer part of the taiko knot double-layered.
- Heko obi Soft with no stiff interface. Usually for children or men.
- Hakata obi Usually silk, with a distinctive pattern. Presented to the Bakufu central government by the Kuroda clan during the Edo period.
- Rokusun obi Size between the hanhaba and hassun. A good choice for someone who is tall.

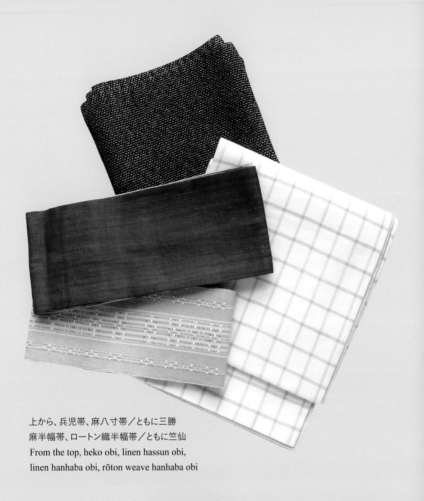

上から、兵児帯、麻八寸帯／ともに三勝
麻半幅帯、ロートン織半幅帯／ともに竺仙
From the top, heko obi, linen hassun obi,
linen hanhaba obi, rōton weave hanhaba obi

博多紗献上帯／丸森
Hakatashakenjo obi

博多紗献上帯／紫織庵
Hakatashakenjo obi

41

協力／井登美

文庫結びを基本に
バリエーションを楽しむ

帯結び七変化

ENJOY DIFFERENT STYLES OF
BUNKO KNOT

OBI KNOT
VARIATIONS

おとなのリボン結び

チェックポイント
Points for a beautiful bow

POINT ①

表に出ている面がす
べて帯の表地になる
ように。

Only the right side of
the fabric shows on
the outside of the obi.

POINT ②

たれ先がヒップをほ
どよくカバー。

The trailing ends fall
to cover the hips.

半幅帯はさまざまな結び方を楽しめる帯です。「文庫結び」(p34〜37)
を基本に、変わり結びに挑戦してみましょう。

You can try a wide variety of knots with a hanhaba obi. Enjoy some
variations of the basic bunko knot (pp. 34-37).

▸ How To

ここまではp35の4までと同じです。
たれを広げます。

The steps are the same up to step 4 on
p.35. Spread out B.

肩幅くらいの幅をとって折ります。

Fold a shoulder-width length (∗).

中心にヒダをつくります。

Pinch the middle together.

ヒダの上にて先を広げます。

Spread out A above the center of the
bow.

▶ How To

て先をヒダにひと巻き、巻き上げます。

Wrap A once around the bow from the bottom.

巻き上げたて先を再び下ろします。

Bring A down again.

5で巻いたところに、て先を途中まで通します。

Insert A half way through the loop you made in step 5.

POINT

リボンをつくるとき、身体側(内側)にくるリボンを両手で引っ張ります。

Pull the front of the loops of the bow with both hands to tighten the knot.

リボンの形をつくります。

Shape the bow.

9

形を整えてリボンの出来上がり。

The finished bow.

10

p37の14と同様に、帯の上と下を持ち、ゆかたの衿合わせに逆らわないように背中心にリボンを回します。

Hold the top and bottom of the obi as in step 14 on p.37 and turn the knot to the back. Turn to the right, same as the yukata overlap.

11

リボンが安定しないときは、たたんだ手ぬぐいなどを胴回りの中心に帯の下から上に向かって入れます。

If the bow is not firmly seated you can insert a small folded towel up under the obi from the bottom.

12

出来上がりです。

Your finished bow.

華やか文庫結び

Fancy Bunko Knot

チェックポイント
Points for a beautiful bow

POINT ①

ふた巻き目でしっか
り巻き上げていれば
緩みません。
Wrap the second time
tightly so the knot
won't come loose.

POINT ②

羽が花びらのように
きれいなヒダに。
The loops of the bow
spread like flower
petals.

かっちりした文庫結びよりもヒダが多く華やかで、世代を問わず人気です。リバーシブルの帯で結ぶとさらに表情豊かに。

With a fancier bow than the standard bunko knot, this is a popular knot for all ages. Reversible fabric is even more gorgeous.

▸ How To

ここまではp35の4までと同じです。

The steps are the same up to step 4 on p.35.

たれを広げて肩幅くらいに折ります。

Spread out B and fold a shoulder-width length (∗).

残りのたれ先を外側に折ります。このとき写真のようにずらしておきます。

Fold the remaining end of B to the outside. Fold it at a slight angle as in the photo.

右手でふたつの羽を押さえながら、ヒダをつくります。

Hold both loops with your right hand and pinch the middle together.

49

▸ How To

ヒダの上にて先を下ろします。

With the pinch on top, bring A down.

て先を羽の上に巻き上げてしっかり締めます。

Wrap A up over the loops and pull tight.

もうひと巻きしてしっかり締めます。

Wrap one more time and pull tight.

て先 A

残りは上に出します。

Pull the remainder up.

て先 A

残ったて先を広げて羽の上に重ねます。

Spread out A and fold on top of the loops of the bow.

羽の形を整えてから、p37の14と同様に、帯の上と下を持ち、ゆかたの衿合わせに逆らわないように背中に回します。

Hold the top and bottom of the obi as in step 14 on p.37 and turn to the back. Turn to the right, same as the yukata overlap.

出来上がりです。

Your finished bow.

変わり錦

にしき

Kawari Nishiki Knot

変わり錦

チェックポイント
Points for a beautiful
kawari nishiki knot

POINT ❶

羽を広げれば華や
かに（写真）、閉じた
まま（p55の8）だと
粋に。

Wide loops look
more fancy (as in the
photo), narrow loops
more chic (step 8 on
p.55).

POINT ❷

ヒップをほどよくカ
バー。

The trailing end falls
to cover the hips.

粋好みでミセスにおすすめの形です。最後の仕上げのバリエーションで粋にも華やかにもなります。

A good choice for a sophisticated, chic look. You can arrange the bow for a more chic or a more fancy impression.

▸ How To

ここまではp34の3までと同じです。たれを三角に折り上げます。

The steps are the same up to step 3 on p.34. Fold B into a triangle.

半分の幅にしたて先とたれを上下入れ替えます。

Cross the folded A down and B up.

ひとつ結びをする要領でたれを途中までくぐらせます。

Bring B up from the bottom as if to tie a knot.

つぎの5で、ここを半分の幅にします
In step 5 you will fold this in half

▶ **How To**

4

て先 A

結び目
Knot

て先を結び目の位置が中心になるように
折ります。

Fold A so that the knot will be at the center.

5

たれ B

とちゅうまでくぐらせたたれを内側に半分
の幅に折って、て先の上に下ろします。

Take B and fold in half lengthwise with the
right side of the fabric on the outside. Bring it
down over the diagonal end from step 4.

6

たれ B

て先 A

下ろしたたれと、て先をひとつ結びします。

Tie B and A with one knot.

7

ひとつ結びしたところ。

After tying the knot.

8

て先を引いて整え、p37の14と同様に、帯の上と下を持ち、ゆかたの衿合わせに逆らわないように背中に回します。

Hold the top and bottom of the obi as in step 14 on p.37 and turn the knot to the back. Turn to the right, same as the yukata overlap.

POINT

粋好みならばこの形で完成。

This is the finished chic look.

9

出来上がりです。

Your finished bow.

協力／紫織庵

自分に似合うアイテム探し
ゆかたを選ぶ、
小物を選ぶ

CHOOSING A YUKATA AND ACCESSORIES
JUST RIGHT
FOR YOU

体型・顔色でゆかたを選ぶ

For Your Body Type and Coloring

背の高い人が似合うゆかた

If you are tall

大柄のゆかたを堂々と着こなすことができるのは背の高い人の特権です。

You can wear bold patterns beautifully.

紫織庵

紫織庵

背の低い人が似合うゆかた

If you are short

愛らしい小柄模様のゆかたを、チャーミングに着こなせます。

Cute, smaller patterns are charming.

井登美

井登美

せっかくのゆかたですから、自分に似合うものを選びたいもの。ここでは体型と顔色別に選び方のポイントをみてみましょう。

You want a yukata that is just right for you. Here's how to choose based on your body type and coloring.

色白の肌に似合うゆかた
If you have fair coloring

明るい色調のゆかたを選ぶと、顔色が健康的にみえます。

A brighter color yukata makes your complexion look fresh and healthy.

井登美

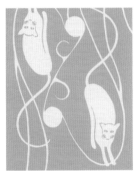

紫織庵

小麦色の肌に似合うゆかた
If you have more tanned coloring

全体的なトーンが、白、ピンク、ブルーなどの薄い色よりも藍色などの濃い色を選ぶとよいでしょう。

You should choose a deep overall tone such as indigo blue rather than a pale tone such as white, pink or blue.

井登美

竺仙

イメージでゆかたを選ぶ

Select Your Image

古きよき時代の感性を受け継ぐ
はんなりゆかた

Traditional Japanese sensibility
Serene but lively yukata

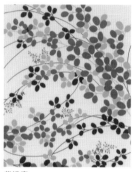

紫織庵

井登美

夏に涼やかに美しく映える
エレガントゆかた

Cool and beautiful
Elegant yukata

竺仙

三勝

60

全身を包むゆかたはその色柄で着る人の雰囲気を演出してくれます。
つぎの夏にまた着るのが楽しみになるような一枚をみつけてください。

The colors and pattern of a full-length yukata express who you are, from head to toe. Find one that you will look forward to wearing again next summer!

女性らしさを際立たせる
かわいいゆかた

Very feminine
Gentle and ladylike yukata

竺仙

井登美

上質なアンティークを装う気分で
レトロモダンゆかた

Sophisticated antique impression
Retro modern yukata

紫織庵

紫織庵

61

通好みの一枚を選ぶ

A Yukata for Connoisseurs

竺仙

奥州小紋
Ōshu komon

手織り紬のような独特の風合いの木綿に、「型染め」を施したものです。

Stencil dyed cotton with the texture of a hand-woven pongee.

竺仙

紅梅小紋
Kōbai komon

格子状に太い糸を織りこんだ木綿に「型染め」を施したものです。独特のシャリ感があります。

Stencil dyed cotton with a lattice texture woven in. Characteristic crisp feel.

竺仙

松煙染小紋
Shōenzome komon

樹脂分の多い松の根をいぶしたすすを松煙といいます。その松煙を使って染めたもので、独特の渋みが特徴です。

Dye made from oxidized resinous pine root gives a quiet, austere impression.

伝統の技を肌で感じることができる逸品は、帯をお太鼓にして、カジュアルな夏のお出かけ着としても活用できます。

An exquisite yukata lets you experience traditional artistry. With an obi tied in a taiko knot you can wear it for a casual summer outing, too.

長板中形
Nagaita chūgata

板の両面に反物を貼りつけ、「型染め」してから藍瓶の中へ浸して染め上げます。裏も表も同じ柄に染まります（p82～83参照）。

The cloth is laid out on both sides of a board for stenciling and then placed in an indigo dye-bath. Both right and wrong sides are dyed with the same pattern.(See pp.82-83)

竺仙

紬
Tsumugi ("pongee")

紬の素朴な風合いを表現した木綿です。軽いデニムのワンピースを着る感覚で挑戦してみては。

The simple texture of cotton pongee – why not wear it as you would a light denim dress?

竺仙

有松鳴海絞り
Arimatsu Narumi shibori

上から「突き出し鹿の子絞り」、「手蜘蛛絞り」、「三浦絞り」。希少な伝統技による逸品（p84参照）。

From the top: tsukidashikanoko pattern, tegumo pattern, Miura pattern. Superb traditional artistry for one-of-a-kind yukata. (See p.84)

近喜

<ruby>一反<rt>いったん</rt></ruby>の<ruby>反物<rt>たんもの</rt></ruby>から生まれる表情

The Impression Starts with a Bolt of Cloth

大胆な柄も帯のセレクト次第で落ち着いた印象にも、より鮮やかにも変身。
／井登美

A bold pattern can create a calm impression or a showier look depending on the obi you choose.

帯や帯留め、合わせる小物でゆかたの印象は大きく変わります。

Your choice of obi, obidome fastener and other accessories can make a big change in the overall impression.

涼しげなゆかたと帯の組み合わせに、帯締めと帯留めで新たな表情をプラス。
／井登美

Add new expression to the cool-looking yukata and obi combination with an obijime tie and obidome fastener.

時代、年齢を問わず人気のゆり柄。紺地に白抜き柄のゆかたで端正な着こなし
に。帯や鼻緒にワンポイントの「赤」を入れてアクセントを。／井登美

A lily pattern, timeless and popular with all ages, in white on an indigo ground creates a
handsome look. Accented with red in the obi and sandal thong.

大正〜昭和につくられた型紙をつかい、配色を変え、今によみがえらせた注染
染めのゆかた。黄色の帯でかわいらしく。／井登美

Stencil patterns from around the 1920s to the 1950s brought back to life with up-to-date
colors. Chūsen dyed yukata. The yellow obi is cute.

ゆかたと帯を合わせる
Yukata and Obi Combinations

生成地に秋の草花を優しく描いたゆかた
Yukata with a delicate pattern of autumn grasses on an unbleached ground

紫織庵

✛ 暖色系の半幅帯
Warm color hanhaba obi

女性らしい優しい印象に。

A gentle, feminine impression.

紫織庵

✛ 抹茶色の半幅帯
Tea green hanhaba obi

渋味のある大人っぽい雰囲気に。

An elegantly simple, adult atmosphere.

帯、帯締め／紫織庵
帯揚げ／井登美

✛ 白の博多紗献上帯
White Hakatasyakenjo obi

同系色で合わせて涼しげで上品なた
たずまいに。

The similar colors create a refreshing,
elegant appearance.

合わせる帯によって一枚のゆかたをさまざまな表情で楽しむことができます。帯でワードローブの幅を広げてみてください。

The same yukata can make many different impressions depending on your choice of obi. Use obi to expand your wardrobe.

シックな奥州小紋のゆかた
Chic Ōshu komon yukata

竺仙

✚ 模様と同系色の半幅帯
Related color hanhaba obi

ターコイズブルーで伝統柄のゆかたを軽やかに。

Turquoise blue makes the traditional pattern light and airy.

竺仙

✚ 薄紫色の半幅帯
Light purple hanhaba obi

ひかえめで優しく上品に。

Reserved and delicately elegant.

竺仙

✚ 紅色の半幅帯
Bright red hanhaba obi

コントラストをつけて若々しく。

Youthful contrast.

69

落ち着いた印象の生成地に桔梗と籠目の伝統模様のゆかた
Yukata with traditional bellflower and basket weave pattern on a sedate unbleached ground

三勝

✚ 薄浅葱色の半幅帯
Ice-blue hanhaba obi

模様と同系色の薄い色で軽やかな印象に。

The lighter related color makes an airy impression.

三勝

✚ 藍色系の縞の半幅帯
Indigo stripe hanhaba obi

模様と同系色の濃い色で落ち着いた印象に。

The darker related color makes a calm impression.

三勝

✚ 濃い京紫色の半幅帯
Deep reddish purple hanhaba obi

京紫色を合わせるとクラシックな雰囲気になります。

Creates a classic atmosphere.

三勝

+ 絞りの兵児帯
A tie-dyed heko obi

兵児帯を変わり結びにすれば個性的
なおしゃれが楽しめます。

A unique and stylish look with the obi
tied in a fancy knot.

三勝

+ ぼかしの入った
桜色の六寸帯
A pink rokusun obi
with gradations

身長が160cm以上の人は、六寸帯
がおすすめ。

A rokusun obi is a good choice if you're
at least 160cm tall.

三勝

+ 麻の八寸帯
A linen hassun obi

お太鼓結びにして、夏のきもの風に。
Tied in a taiko knot, it's like a summer
kimono.

ゆかたを夏きものとして着る

Yukata as Summer Kimono

いつものゆかた
Your usual yukata

井登美

紫織庵

夏きものに
Now a summer kimono

涼しげな楊柳の半衿をつけ、三分紐と
花の帯留め、帯揚げをプラス。同系色
で甘くまとめました。／井登美

A cool crepe inner collar, sanbu ("9 mm")
tie and flower fastener, with obiage cloth.
Related colors gently unite the look.

絽の半衿をつけ、博多紗献上帯をお太
鼓結びに。帯締め、帯揚げは帯と溶け
合う色でエレガントに。／紫織庵

A silk gauze inner collar and
Hakatasyakenjo obi tied in a taiko knot. The
objime tie and obiage cloth colors blend
with the obi for an even more elegant look.

肌着を兼ねた半襦袢に衿をつけ足袋をはけば、いつものゆかたも涼やかな夏ものになります。

With an inner collar on the underwear top and tabi socks on your feet, your yukata becomes a cool summer kimono.

三勝

井登美

絽の半衿をつけ、バラの花色よりも柔らかい色調の帯締めと帯揚げをプラスして優しく。／三勝

A silk gauze inner collar, with soft rose obijime tie and obiage cloth create a delicate look.

絽の半衿をつけ、濃藍の紗八寸帯でキリリとした装いに。帯締めと帯揚げはなじむ色を選んで。／井登美

A silk gauze inner collar, deep indigo gauze hassun obi for a clean cut look. Choose an obijime tie and obiage cloth in colors that blend.

73

ゆかたの周りの愛らしい小物たち

Lovely Accessories for Your Yukata

帯締め
おびじ
—— Obijime tie ——

帯の上に最後に締める紐です。帯留めをつけたい人は
三分紐、二分紐といわれる細い紐を使うのが一般的で
さんぶひも　にぶひも
す。小さな面積ですが、帯締め一本でコーディネート全
体の雰囲気を左右します。

The obijime is tied over your obi. If you want to add a
fastener, a narrow sanbu ("9 mm") or nibu ("6 mm") tie
is a good choice. It's not very wide, but it can change the
whole look.

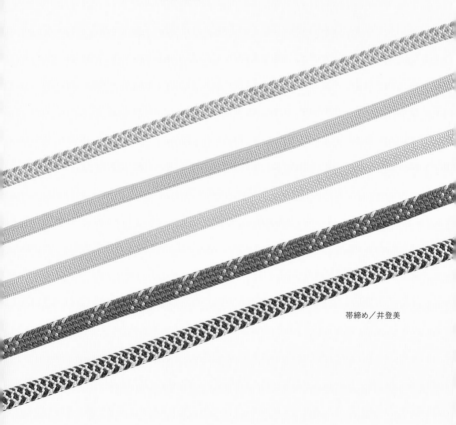

帯締め／井登美

ゆかたと半幅帯のシンプルなコーディネートも素敵ですが、ときにはアクセサリー感覚で小物をプラスすると、おしゃれ心がトキメキます。

You can create a simple combination with yukata and hanhaba obi, but adding accessories sometimes can thrill your sense of fashion.

帯留め
おびどめ
Obidome fastener

帯締めの中央につけるアクセサリーの一種です。体の中心にくるので、小さくても人の視線を集めます。ゆかたには銀細工、ガラス細工、陶器など夏の素材感たっぷりのものを。

The fastener goes in the center of your obi, so even though it is small it attracts a lot of attention. Choose a summery silver, glass or ceramic fastener for your yukata.

帯留め／井登美

帯揚げ
（おびあ）

Obiage
cloth

ゆかたの周りの愛らしい小物たち

お太鼓結びにしたときに帯枕にかけて使いますが、半幅帯を結ぶときにも装飾的に使うことができます。見える部分はほんの少しですが、コーディネートの大事な役割を果たします。きものや帯に使用されている柄から一色をとると失敗しません。素材は絽、または楊柳などがおすすめです。長いストールで代用することもできます。

The cloth is used to cover the obimakura cushion when tying your obi in a taiko knot, but you can also add it as a decoration when tying a hanhaba obi. Only a bit is visible, but it plays a big role in the overall look. Select a color in your yukata or obi and you won't go wrong. Silk gauze or crepe are a good choice of fabric. You can also use a long stole.

これがお太鼓結び。「きちんと感」もでて大人っぽい雰囲気に。

The taiko knot creates an adult, pulled-together feeling.

上は絽帯揚げ、下2枚は紗ぼかし帯揚げ／井登美

Top is silk gauze. Bottom two are gauze with gradations.

半衿
はんえり
Inner collar

本来はきものの衿の汚れを防ぐために襦袢の衿にかけておくものです。顔に近いので、顔映りがよいかどうかが大切なポイント。素材は絽か楊柳、または手ぬぐいなどの木綿も。

This is added to the underwear to keep the kimono collar clean. This collar is near your face, so an important point is how it flatters your complexion. Fabrics include silk gauze, crepe or cotton tenugui.

上から、ぼかしが入った麻半衿、刺しゅう入り麻半衿、下は絽の半衿。／井登美

From the top, linen with gradations, embroidered linen, bottom is silk gauze.

手ぬぐい
Tenugui

ハンカチの代わりとして、また帯が緩んだときに帯の中に入れたりなど持っていると便利です。小紋柄ならば半衿代わりに使うこともできます。

You can use a tenugui instead of a handkerchief, or put it inside your obi if it starts to get loose. If the pattern is small you can also use it as an inner collar.

手ぬぐい／紫織庵

かごバッグ
Basket bag

涼感のあるかごバッグは、ゆかたとの相性がバツグンです。山葡萄_{やまぶどう}のつるで編んだ上等なものなら長く使えます。内袋の素材や模様にもこだわって選びましょう。

Basket bags give the same cool feeling as yukata. A fine quality bag made of wild grapevine lasts a lifetime. Choose the inner fabric and pattern carefully.

かごバッグ／井登美

ゆかたの周りの愛らしい小物たち

日傘_{ひがさ}
Parasol

昼間のお出かけには、日傘を持ちましょう。紫外線を防いでくれると同時に、ゆかた姿が絵のように決まります。

Take a parasol if you go out in the daytime. It will protect you from UV rays and create a picturesque impression at the same time.

日傘／井登美

かんざし
Kanzashi hairpin

まとめ髪のアクセントとしてマストアイテムです。後ろ姿にまで心配りを。

This is a must as an accent for an upswept hairstyle. Pay attention to how you look from the back, too.

かんざし／井登美

根(ね)つけ
Netsuke

帯の間に差しこんで使います。歩くたびに揺れるかわいいアクセサリー。

Tuck the end in your obi. This cute accessory swings as you walk.

根つけ／井登美

79

表が畳表の下駄
たたみおもて
Tatami insole

裏にラバーが
貼られた下駄
Rubber soles

塗の下駄
Lacquered

下駄／井登美

下駄
げた
Geta clogs

高さや台の形、素材、鼻緒の素材や色柄などさまざまな
はなお
種類があります。実際にはいてみて、足の形に合うかど
うかを確認して選びましょう。鼻緒の色で迷う場合は白
っぽいものだとどんな色柄のゆかたにも似合います。ま
た、歩くと音がする下駄は、フォーマルな場には向きま
せん。

You can choose from many types of sole height, shape and
material, and thong color, pattern and material. Be sure to
try them on and make sure they fit. If you are not sure what
color thong you want, a shade of white will go with any
color yukata. Geta make a sound as you walk, so they are
not suitable for formal occasions.

足袋
Tabi socks

ゆかたは素足でOKですが、半
衿をつけたり、帯をお太鼓結び
にしたときは足袋をはくときもの
らしくなります。夏は麻が涼し
げですが、レースの足袋なども
おしゃれです。

You can go barefoot, but if you
are wearing an inner collar or
have your obi tied in a taiko
knot, tabi socks add to the
kimono look. Linen socks are
cool in summer, but lace are
stylish, too.

レース足袋／井登美

足が痛くならない下駄選び、歩き方のコツ
How to choose geta clogs and walk comfortably

足が痛くならないよう、下駄は、足の甲
に当たる側の鼻緒がふっくらしているも
のを選びます。はくときは、足の親指と
人差し指で前緒をつまんではきます。こ
のとき前緒がしっかりしまっていると指
がほどよく固定され、歩くのが楽になり
ます。前緒が緩いと、指が遊んでしまい、
すれて痛みの原因になります。前緒が
緩いと思ったら履物屋さんで詰めても
らいましょう。

Choose geta clogs with a soft, thick thong.
Put them on with the short, vertical part of
the thong between your large toe and the
next toe. If the thong fits securely and holds
your toes comfortably in place, you can
walk comfortably. If the thong is too loose
and your toes move around, the chafing may
cause pain. If you feel the thong is loose,
take them to a shoe shop and get them
adjusted.

前緒
Thong between the toes

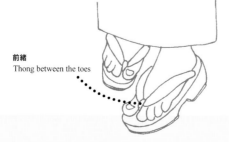

ゆかたの染めを学ぶ
How Yukata Are Dyed

　美しく染められたゆかたには、伝統を受け継いだ職人たちの熟練した技と、ていねいな仕事が息づいています。数多くあるゆかた染めのなか、つぎの3つを紹介します。

The master skills of traditional artisans come to life in beautifully dyed yukata. Here are three of the many techniques used to dye yukata.

注染
Chūsen

反物を手ぬぐいの大きさにたたみ折り、柄の部分に染液を一気に流しこんで染める染色方法です。一度に多色を使って大量に染めることができます。また染料が布の下側に抜けるため、布の芯まで美しく染まり、表裏同じ濃さになります。にじみやぼかしを生かした模様もでき、情緒のある布になります。手ぬぐいの多くもこの技法で染められます。

The cloth is folded into the size of tenugui hand towels and the dye is poured over the pattern. Many colors can be used at once time to dye a large amount of fabric. The dye goes all the way through to the other side of the fabric, so even the center of the cloth is beautifully dyed, with right and wrong sides of the cloth in the same shade of color. Patterns can use blurring and gradation for expressive fabric. This method is used for most tenugui hand towels.

長板中形
Nagaita chūgata

型染め染色の一種です。中形とは模様を表す言葉で、小紋、大紋の真ん中くらいの大きさの模様のことで、ゆかたの代名詞ともなっています。長さ約6.5mの板の上に反物を置き、おもに伊勢で彫られた型紙を置いて型染めをしていきます。地色を藍にして模様を白く染め抜くものと、白地に藍で模様を染めていく方法があります。

One method of stencil dyeing, "chūgata" refers to the size of the pattern, mid-way between large and small patterns, which is typical for yukata. Cloth is laid out on a 6.5 meter board and stenciled, usually with paper stencils cut in Ise. There are white patterns on an indigo ground and indigo patterns on a white ground.

注染 Chūsen

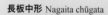

写真協力／中川染工場

長板中形 Nagaita chūgata

写真協力／松原伸生

有松鳴海絞り
Arimatsu Narumi shibori

安藤広重の「東海道五十三次」にも登場する有松鳴海。その町で生み出された絞り染めは、尾張徳川家の保護を受け発展しました。布をつまんで糸で巻く、ヒダをとって糸で縫う、棒に布を巻きつけてその布を押し縮めるなどの工程を経て染めたあと、糸を解くと独特の模様が現れます。職人が一生のうちに絞る技は1種類のみ。現在でも70種類以上の技が伝承されています。

Arimatsu Narumi is one of Hiroshige's "53 Stations of the Tokaido". The dye technique that originated there developed under the protection of the Owari Tokugawa family. The cloth is gathered and bound with thread, sewn into folds, or wrapped around a pole and gathered together and then dyed. The characteristic tie-dye patterns are revealed when the cloth is opened up. An artisan will spend a whole lifetime on a single technique. Currently there are more than 70 techniques being handed down.

写真協力／
竹田嘉兵衛商店

有松鳴海絞り
Arimatsu Narumi shibori

協力／井登美

協力／紫織庵

CHAPTER

きちんと粋に着る
男ゆかたの着方

WITH A CLEAN, CHIC LOOK

MEN'S
YUKATA

準備するもの
What You Need for Wearing a Yukata

肌襦袢
はだじゅばん
Hadajuban
underwear top

肌に優しく、通気性・吸湿性・速
乾性に富んだ自然素材の半袖タ
イプを選びましょう。洋服用のVネ
ック肌着（半袖）でも代用できます。
／井登美

A short-sleeve top in a natural fabric is
breathable, absorbent, fast drying and
kind to your skin. You can also wear a
short-sleeve V-neck undershirt.

肌着
Underwear

ステテコ
Suteteko underwear bottom

汗によるベタつきを防ぎ、足さばき
をよくしてくれるので必ず着用しま
しょう。／井登美

Japanese style long drawers are cool
and comfortable, and keep the yukata
from clinging to your legs.

腰紐
こしひも
Koshihimo
sash

1本あれば大丈夫です。
You only need one.

88

男ゆかたもきちんと下着を着用しましょう。汗をかいても快適、ゆかたへの汚れも防いでくれます。

The right underwear makes all the difference. You'll be comfortable and your yukata will stay fresh even on the hottest days.

巾着
Kinchaku drawstring pouch

布や革でできていて口を紐で縛って持ちます。和装ならではの粋な小物です。／紫織庵

Kinchaku pouches are available in cloth or leather. A truly Japanese fashion accessory.

男ゆかたの こだわり小物
Men's accessories

かかとが低いタイプ。鼻緒と台の組み合わせで個性を楽しめます。／井登美

Low heeled type. Many unique combinations of sole and thong for you to choose among.

2枚歯タイプ。歩くとカランコロンという音がします。ホテルなどフォーマルな場所では控えましょう。／井登美

Geta with two teeth. These make a pleasant clacking sound as you walk, but avoid them at hotels or other formal occasions.

下駄
Geta wooden clogs

台の素材、高さ、鼻緒の色柄などさまざまな種類があります。まずははいてみて、鼻緒は痛くないかなど足に合うか確認しましょう。かかとがすこし出るくらいがちょうどよいサイズです。

You can choose from many kinds of sole, height and thong color and pattern. Be sure to try them on and make sure they fit and the thong is not too tight. Your heel should hang over a bit.

足に優しい畳表の下駄。／井登美

Geta with tatami surface are kind to your feet.

89

男ゆかたの着つけ
「きちんと」「きれいに」のコツ

Men's Yukata — tips and pointers for a clean, chic look

▸ **How To**

1

ゆかたを羽織り、下前を合わせます。

Put the yukata on. Bring the right side over.

2

上前を合わせます。

Bring the left top side over the right.

3

腰紐を下腹に当てます。

Place the koshihimo sash below your waistline at the hips.

女性のゆかたと違い、おはしょりの処理がないぶん、慣れれば簡単に着ることができます。粋に着こなしましょう。

Unlike women's yukata, you don't need to make the ohashori fold, so it's simple to learn. Go for a chic look!

4 後ろに回して交差しながら締めます。

Cross the sash in back as you pull it tight.

5 腰紐を前に回して、自分から見て左の紐を上にして交差させます。

Bring the sash around to the front and cross the left-hand end over the right.

6 2回絡げて締めます。

Wrap around twice and pull tight.

POINT

きちんと締めます。
Pull tight.

▶ How To

下になっているほうの紐を折って
輪にします。

Make a loop with the bottom end.

上になっていた紐を輪の上からか
けて、輪の下からくぐらせ、左に抜
きとります。

Bring the upper end down over the
loop and then pass it through the loop
from below out to the left.

しっかり締めます。

Pull tight.

長いほうの紐端は巻いている腰紐
にはさんで留めます。つぎは帯を
締めます。

Tuck the long end under the sash.
Next you'll tie the obi.

帯結びの基本
貝の口の結び方
Kai-no-kuchi — basic obi knot

男性の角帯を使ったもっともポピュラーな結び方です。きものと同じなので、覚えておくときものでも活躍します。

The most popular knot for a men's kaku obi. You can use the same knot when wearing a kimono.

▸ **How To**

角帯を持ち、先端の40cmくらいを半分の幅に折ります。こちらがて先になります。

Fold about 40 cm of one end of the obi in half lengthwise. This is the tesaki (A).

1で折ったて先を体の中心に当てて巻いていきます。3巻きします。

Place A at the center of your body and wrap the obi around three times.

3巻きしたら、残ったたれ側の帯を、右腕を45度に伸ばしたぐらいの長さにとって、身体に折りこみます。

Take a length of the remaining tare (B) with your right arm at a 45° angle and fold that to the inside.

て先を下にして交差させます。交差の位置は、体の中心よりもすこし横にずらします。

Bring A down and cross with B on top. The cross should be slightly off your center line.

93

▸ **How To**

ひとつ結びにして締めます。

Tie once and pull tight.

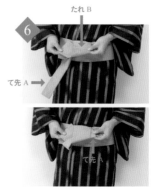

たれ B

て先 A

て先 A

上になったたれ側の帯を下ろして
から、身体側に折りこんで輪をつく
り、そこにて先を通します。

Bring B down and fold to the inside to
make a loop. Pass A through the loop.

しっかり結びます。

Tie tightly.

右回転で背中に回して、出来上が
りです。

Turn the obi to the right until the knot
is at the back, and your obi is finished.

仕上げのチェック
粋なゆかた姿のポイント
Final Check Points for a Chic Look

前の仕上がり
Front

POINT

① 衿合わせはゆったりと。
Collars loosely overlapped.

② 帯は下腹の位置から、やや後ろ上がりに締めます。
Obi is low in front angling up slightly in back.

③ 前裾はすこし斜めに上げ気味に。
Front of the hem slightly up on the diagonal.

後ろの仕上がり
Back

POINT

④ 背中はすこしダブついてるくらいでOKです。
The back can be a bit baggy.

⑤ 結び目は身体の中心線より少し横にずらします。
The knot is slightly off center.

⑥ て先がすこし長いぐらいが粋に見えます。
The tesaki looks chic a little longer than the tare.

ゆかた、帯／紫織庵

一文字結び

Ichimonji Knot

▸ How To

ここまでは貝の口結びの2（p93）
までと同じです。

The steps are the same as kai-no-kuchi
up to step 2 on p.93.

たれ側を三角に折り上げます。

Fold B into a triangle.

ひとつ結びにします。

Tie once.

ひとつ結びにしたて先とたれを垂
直にします。

Hold the ends straight up and down.

形はリボンですが、女性のものとは違い、小さく一文字にまっすぐ結びます。キリリとした印象に仕上げましょう。

A type of bow with a small straight knot, differing from the women's knot. Go for a clean look.

5

上になったて先を帯に預けるか、クリップで留めます。

Lay A over the obi or hold in place with a clip.

← て先 A

6

たれ側の結び目に近いところを広げます。

Spread out B.

← たれ B

7

体の横幅半分（帯幅の2〜3倍）ぐらいの長さをとって折りこみます。

Fold a length about half the width of your body (2-3 times the width of the obi).

▸ How To

8

真ん中で半分に折ります。

Fold in half.

9

て先 A

たれ B

クリップをはずし、て先を中心に下ろします。

Take off the clip. Bring A over the center of B.

10

て先 A

て先を羽の裏に回します。

Wrap A behind the bow.

11

そして、左に抜きとります。

And pull up to the left.

ここでしっかり締めます。

Pull tight.

て先 A

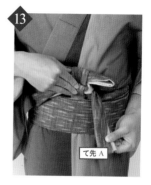

て先 A

て先を下に下ろします。

Bring A down.

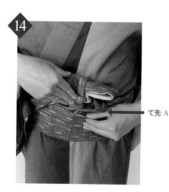

て先 A

帯の2巻目と3巻目のあいだに、て
先を入れます。

Insert A between the second and third
layers of the obi.

て先 A

そのて先を下に引き出します。

Pull A down.

‣ How To

16

帯を右方向に回転させ、背中の中心に結び目を移動させます。

Turn the obi to the right until the knot is at the back.

17

下に出ているて先を巻き上げていきます。

Roll the remainder of A up under the obi.

て先 A

18

帯の真ん中にくるくらいまで巻き上げて完成です。

Roll up to the center of the obi.

仕上げのチェック
粋なゆかた姿のポイント
Final Check Points for a Chic Look

前の仕上がり
Front

POINT 1

前帯は下腹からやや
後ろ上がりに締めます。
Obi is low in front
angling up slightly in
back.

後ろの仕上がり
Back

POINT 2

結び目は背中心です。
Knot is centered.

POINT 3

て先を巻き込んでいる
部分に帯がしっかりの
っています。
Tesaki bow sits securely
on top of the obi.

日本の模様を知る
Japanese Textile Patterns

　古くから日本人は四季折々の動植物や風景を
きものの模様に映しだしてきました。その豊かな
感性とデザイン力は、現代になってもなお揺る
ぎないものがあります。日本の代表的な模様を
紹介します。

Traditionally Japanese have decorated their
kimono with plants and animals and scenes
of the four seasons. That rich sensibility
and skill in design endures today. Here are
some representative traditional patterns.

動物・植物模様
Plants and animals

松 Pine

蝶 Butterfly

竹 Bamboo

その他 Other

桜 Cherry
花唐草 Flower arabesque
花の丸 Flower circle
秋草 Autumn grasses
燕 Swallow
唐花 Arabesque
千鳥 Plover

自然・風景模様
Nature and landscapes

月 Moon

波 Waves

雪輪 Snowflakes

その他 Other

水 Water

青海波 Overlapping waves

ゑがすみ
ゑ霞 Mist

かんぜすい
観世水 Flowing water

滝 Waterfall

雪花 Snowflower

ちゃやつじ
茶屋辻 Water garden

器物模様
Objects

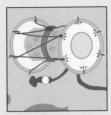

つづみ
鼓 Drum

ひょうたん
瓢箪 Gourd

せんめん
扇面 Fan

その他 Other

鈴 Bell

のし
熨斗 Decorative tie

そうし
冊子 Booklet

げんじこう
源氏香 Genji incense

かさ
笠 Straw hat

花籠 Flower basket

楽器 Musical instrument

幾何学模様
Geometric

いちまつ
市松 Check

たすき
襷 Tasuki diamond

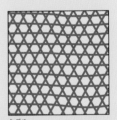

かごめ
籠目 Basket weave

その他 Other

麻の葉 Hemp leaf

うろこ
鱗 Scales

鍵 Key pattern

あじろ
網代 Wicker

まつかわびし
松皮菱 Pine bark diamond

よろけ縞 Wavy stripe

格子 Lattice

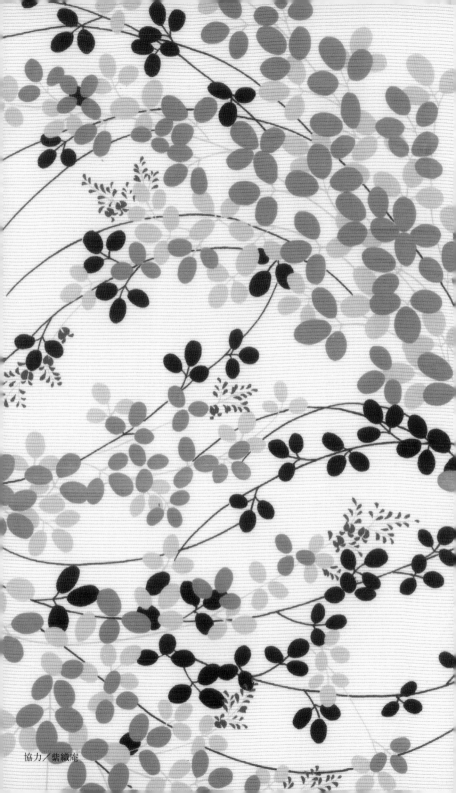

協力／紫織庵

SOS対策と立ち居振る舞い

美しく着こなすために

WHEN IT STARTS TO COME APART
AND GOOD MANNERS

WEARING
YUKATA
BEAUTIFULLY

着くずれSOS

When It Starts to Come Apart

こんなふうに
着くずれてしまったら!?
SOS – your yukata is
coming apart!

CHECK ①

衿がゆるゆるに!
➡P107

Collar is gaping.
(p.107)

CHECK ④

おはしょりがグチャ
グチャ!
➡P108

Ohashori fold is
crumpled. (p.108)

CHECK ③

脇のあたりがダボダ
ボになってしまった!
➡P108

Sides are baggy.
(p.108)

CHECK ⑤

後ろの帯が落ちてき
てしまった!
➡P109

Your obi is drooping
in back. (p.109)

CHECK ②

裾を踏んでしまった!
➡P107

You're stepping on
your hem. (p.107)

動いているうちに着くずれてしまうことはよくあることです。そんなとき慌てないためにも着くずれ直しのコツを覚えておきましょう。

Your yukata will often start to come apart as you move around. Remember these tips to recover a pulled-together look.

衿を直す
Fixing your collar

POINT

反対の衿は、ダブついている分を帯の上から中に入れこむ。

Flatten the other side of the collar by tucking it into the obi from above.

直したいほうの衿を、手でたどりながら衿山のラインを整えていきます。

Run your fingers along the collar to straighten it out.

おはしょりの下に出ている衿先を引っ張り、ゆるみをとります。

Pull down the end of the collar under the ohashori fold to flatten it.

裾を直す
Fixing the hem

適正な裾の位置を確認して手で押さえます。

Hold the hem in the right position.

帯の下に出ているおはしょりをめくって、裾が適正な位置にくるまで腰紐の上のおはしょりを引き上げます。

Lift up the ohashori fold under the obi and pull it up over the koshihimo tie until the hem is in the right position.

おはしょりの下線を反対側の脇に向かってすこしずつ引き上げながら整えます。

Lift it up a little at a time with the bottom of the ohashori fold angled toward the other side.

脇を直す
Fixing the sides

帯の下に出ているおはしょりを下に引きます。

Pull down the ohashori fold under the obi.

おはしょりの下線が帯の下線と平行になるように整え、余分は帯の中に入れこみます。

Bring the bottom of the ohashori fold even with the obi, tucking the excess into the obi.

おはしょりを直す
Fixing the ohashori fold

おはしょりの下線をまず帯と平行になるように整えます。

Bring the bottom of the ohashori fold even with the obi.

おはしょりのあまりを脇に向かってすこしずつ寄せて、帯の中に下から入れこみます。

Bring any excess over to your side a little at a time. Tuck it into the obi from below.

帯を上げる
Lifting the obi

タオルやハンカチ、手ぬぐいなどを
折って丸めます。

Roll up a small towel, handkerchief or
tenugui hand towel.

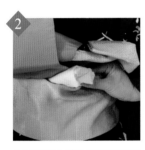

たれを持ち上げて、結び目の下の
帯の中に入れます。

Lift up the knot and tuck it into the obi
under the fold.

帯の結び目を2の上にのせます。

Lift the knot of the obi to sit on top of
the towel.

きれいに直りました!
Now it's fixed!

美しい立ち居振る舞い

Beautiful Manners

歩く
Walking

歩く前に裾を開いて、下前を折り
返しておきます。

Before you start, open the skirt and
rewrap the right side.

体の重心を前に置くような気持ち
で歩きます。

Keep your center of balance slightly
forward as you walk.

階段を上る
Climbing stairs

裾を踏みやすいので、片手で上前
を持ちましょう。

Lift the left side with one hand so you
don't step on your hem.

タクシーを呼ぶ
Calling a taxi

手を上げるときは、腕が出ないよう
に、反対の手で袖口の下を押さえ
ます。

Use the other hand to hold your sleeve
to keep your arm covered.

美しくゆかたを着たら、立ち居振る舞いにも気を配りたいもの。いくつか
のコツと所作を紹介します。

When you wear a beautiful yukata you want beautiful manners, too. Here
are some pointers.

椅子に座る
Sitting in a chair

椅子の左横に立ち、左足
を斜め前に出します。

Stand to the left of the
chair. Move your left leg
forward on the diagonal.

右足で椅子の前に体を
もっていきます。

With your right leg bring
yourself in front of the
chair.

左足をそろえます。

Bring your left leg next to
your right.

上前をすこし上げます。

Lift the left side of your
yukata slightly.

きものの後ろに手を添え
て座ります。

Sit using your hands at the
back to keep the yukata
smooth.

背もたれからすこし空間
をあけて座ります。

Leave some space between
your back and the backrest.

バッグを置く
Putting down your bag

背もたれとの空間に置きます。

Put your bag between your back and the backrest.

テーブルの上の物をとる
Taking something from the table

袖がテーブルにつかないように、もう片方の手で袖口の下を押さえます。

Use the other hand to hold your sleeve so it doesn't brush the table.

ストローで飲む
Drinking from a straw

コップの下を指先で持ち、もう片方の手をストローに添え、口にもっていきます。

Hold the glass with your fingertips. Hold the straw with your other hand and bring it to your mouth.

コーヒーカップで飲む
Drinking from a coffee cup

カップの取っ手を指先でつまんで持ち上げて、口に運びます。

Hold the handle with your fingertips and bring it to your mouth.

NG集
What Not to Do

これはマナー違反！気をつけましょう。
Bad manners! Be careful.

足を開く。

Sitting with your legs apart.

足を組む。

Crossing your legs.

椅子の背にもたれる。

Leaning back in your chair.

コップを持たず顔をストローに近づける。

Bringing your mouth to the straw without holding the glass in your hand.

片手で飲む。

Using only one hand to drink.

取っ手に指をくぐらせ親指を上に出す。

Hooking your fingers through the cup handle with your thumb on top.

ゆかたの汗じみ対策

Getting Rid of Sweat Stains

汗をかくまえに「汗とり」でシミ予防

Use pads to protect your yukata before you wear it

脇の下
Underarms

タオルや手ぬぐい（さらし、ガーゼだと
なおよい）を半円に断ち、下着の脇に内
側から縫いつけます（外側でもかまいま
せん）。

Cut a towel or tenugui hand towel (bleached
cotton or gauze is good) in a half-circle
and sew under the arms of your underwear
top on the inside (on the outside is also
possible).

背中
Back

タオルなどを下着の後ろ衿の幅、腰の
上ぐらいまでの長さに断ち、衿の内側に
縫いつけます。

Cut a towel the same width as the back
collar of your underwear top and long
enough to reach the top of your hips. Sew it
inside your collar.

おなか
Stomach

下着の上から折ったタオルをウエスト
にひと巻きします（イラスト）。また汗と
り専用の肌着もあります（写真）。

Wrap a folded towel once around your
waist over your underwear. There are also
underwear specially made to absorb sweat.

商品協力／井登美

114

大切なゆかたを汗じみから守りましょう。

Protect your yukata from sweat.

汗をかいたあとのお手入れ
After wearing

乾いたバスタオルの上に汗でぬれた部分を置き、水をかたく絞ったタオルで上からトントンとたたき、汗をバスタオルに移動させます。

Place the sweaty part on top of a dry bath towel and tap with a slightly damp hand towel.

衣紋かけにつるして乾かします。

Dry on a hanger.

それでも気になる場合は洗いましょう(p122〜125参照)。

If that is not enough, wash the yukata (see pp.122-125).

季節の終わりにはクリーニング屋さんや呉服屋さんで洗ってもらうと安心です。

You can have a dry cleaner or kimono shop clean your yukata at the end of the season for no worries.

ゆかたにシミをつけてしまったら

水性のシミ
Water soluble stains

ゆかたによっては水で色落ちして
しまうものがあるので、注意しなが
ら行いましょう。まずは乾いたハン
カチの上にシミのついた部分をの
せ、水分を含んだタオルなどで表
からトントンとたたいてハンカチに
汚れを移していきます。その後アイ
ロンで乾かしますが、アイロンがな
い場合は、両手のひらを当てて乾
かします。

Some yukata may fade if washed with
water, so take care when removing the
stain. Start by laying the stain over a
dry handkerchief and tapping with a
damp towel. You can dry the yukata
with an iron, or with the warmth of
your hands if you are not at home.

汗、コーヒー、紅茶、ワイン、醤油、血液など

Sweat, coffee, tea, wine, soy sauce and blood are
examples of water soluble stains.

116

シミが水性か油性かによって対処法も異なります。ケース別に応急処置をみていきましょう。

Water soluble and oil soluble stains need different treatment. Let's look at what to do for each type.

油性のシミ
Oil soluble stains

素人ではきれいに落とすことができません。まずはティッシュなどで水分をとって汚れが広がらないようにします。その後、クリーニング屋さん、または呉服屋さんに持って行きましょう。

These stains need to be handled by a professional. Use a tissue to blot any liquid so the stain does not spread. Then take your yukata to the dry cleaner or kimono shop.

口紅、ファンデーション、ケチャップ、ソース、チョコレートなど

Lipstick, foundation, ketchup, Worcestershire sauce and chocolate are examples of oil soluble stains.

保管中に黄ばみが出てしまったら
Yellowing during storage

漂白剤は使用できません。黄ばみはプロでもきれいに落とすことはできませんが、クリーニング屋さん、または呉服屋さんに相談してみましょう。汚れを放置することで黄ばみができるので、きれいに洗ってからしまうことが大事です。

Do NOT use bleach. Even a professional cannot completely remove these stains, but consult with your dry cleaner or kimono shop. Yellowing can be caused by storing the yukata without cleaning it first, so it's important to clean it properly before putting it away.

117

写真に素敵に写るコツ
Looking Good in a Photo

　ゆかたが上手に着られるようになったら、写真に撮って思い出に残したいもの。洋服とはちょっと違う、きれいに写真に写るコツがあります。ぜひ試してみてください。

You want to have a beautiful photo of yourself wearing yukata. Looking good in a photo is a bit different from Western clothes, so try these tips.

椅子に腰かけて写真を撮るとき
Sitting in a chair

STEP 1

体の向きはやや斜め。顔のみカメラに向けます。

Sit at a slight angle. Only your face should be turned toward the camera.

STEP 3

反っくり返らず、体はやや前に。背筋は伸ばします。

Don't lean back, lean slightly forward. Keep your back straight and your head held high.

STEP 2

浅く座ります。

Sit forward in the chair.

STEP 4

両足は自然に斜めにそろえて、かかとを上げ気味にします。

Your feet are naturally at an angle, with your heels slightly up.

STEP ②

顔だけカメラに向け
ます。

Only your face should
be turned toward the
camera.

STEP ③

背筋を伸ばします。お
なかを引っこめ、胸を
出す気持ちで立ちます。

Stomach in, chest
slightly out. Keep
your back straight
and your head held
high.

STEP ⑤

両足をそろえて立ち、
つま先はそろえたま
ま、かかとを握りこぶ
しひとつ分開きます。

With your feet
together, keep your
toes together and
open your heels about
the width of a fist.

立ち姿を
写真に撮るとき
Standing

STEP ①

体はカメラに対し斜
め45度に。

Stand at a 45 degree
angle from the
camera.

STEP ④

前になった左足に重
心をかけます。

Place your weight on
your left foot in front.

STEP ⑥

右足を左足の土踏
まずのあたりまで後
ろに引く（逆向きのと
きは反対の足を）。

Bring your right foot
back to about the arch
of the left foot (or the
opposite if your body
is angled the other
way).

119

協力／井登美

ゆかたを着たあとに
ゆかたのお手入れと
しまい方

AFTER YOU WEAR YOUR YUKATA
CARE AND
STORAGE

ゆかたの洗い方
Cleaning Your Yukata

洗濯の前に
Before machine washing

衿の部分が動かないように縫います。ざくざく縫いで大丈夫です。

Sew the collar in place. Large basting stiches are fine.

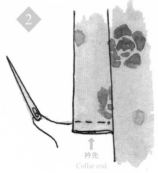

衿先
Collar end

衿先も同様に縫います。

Sew the collar ends, too.

歯ブラシなどに洗剤をつけて、衿、袖口などを部分洗いしておきます。

Put some detergent on an old toothbrush and pre-wash the collar and edges of the sleeves.

ゆかたをたたみ、三つ折りにします。たたみ方はp126〜131参照。

Fold the yukata into thirds.
See pp.126-131.

木綿のゆかたは家庭の洗濯機で洗うことができます。色落ちが心配な場合は、目立たないところを水に通して確認してから洗いましょう。

Cotton yukata can be cleaned in your washing machine. If you are worried about the colors fading, try testing with water in an inconspicuous place first.

洗濯機で洗う
Machine washing

洗濯ネットに入れます。

Put the yukata in a laundry net.

普通の洗剤を入れて、ソフトモードや手洗いモードで洗います。脱水にはかけません。

Use your regular detergent in the delicate or hand-wash cycle. Do not use a spin cycle.

形をくずさないように洗濯ネットから出して、バスタオルにはさみます。

Take the yukata out of the net without unfolding and place inside a towel.

くるくると巻いて水分をとります。

Roll up the towel to squeeze out the water.

干す
Hanging

物干しざおなどにかけて、縫い目に寄った
シワを引っ張ってとります。

Pass the sleeves through a laundry pole and
smooth out any wrinkles at the seams.

衿などはたたいてシワをとります。

Pat the collar to take out the wrinkles.

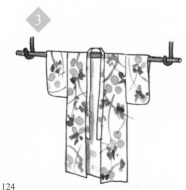

そのまま半乾きになるまで干します。

Hang until half-dry.

アイロンをかける場合
If you iron your yukata

衿からアイロンをかけます。

Start ironing from the collar.

たたみながらアイロンをかけていきます。たたみ方はp126〜131参照。

Fold as you iron. See pp.126-131 for how to fold.

アイロンをかけない場合
If you don't iron your yukata

ゆかたをたたんで三つ折りにし、乾いたバスタオルにはさみ、上下にビニールを敷きます。

Fold the yukata into thirds. Place inside a dry towel. Put between two pieces of plastic.

上に座布団2枚くらいの重しをのせてひと晩おきます。翌日、また物干しなどにかけて干します。

Weigh down with two or three cushions on top and leave overnight. Hang again the next day on a laundry pole until fully dry.

ゆかたのたたみ方

Folding Your Yukata

▸ **How To**

自分の体に対して、衿側が左、裾側が右
になるように、平行にゆかたを置きます。

Place the neck of the yukata to your left and
the bottom of the yukata to your right and lay
it out evenly.

手前の脇縫いで手前の身頃が向こう側に
きちんと折れているか確認します。

Make sure that the front side of the yukata
close to you is neatly folded at the side seam.

POINT

手のひらを裾の方向に動かしながら、
空気を抜く。空気が入ったままたたむ
とシワの原因に。

Use the palm of your hand to smooth
the air out down toward the bottom. Air
will cause wrinkles.

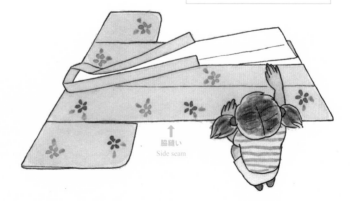

↑
脇縫い
Side seam

126

ゆかたを脱いだらその瞬間からつぎに着るときの準備が始まっています。
たたみ方のポイントはシワをつくらないこと。ていねいにたたみましょう。

As soon as you take off your yukata you are starting to get it ready to wear
again. Fold it carefully so there will be no wrinkles the next time.

身頃を衽の縫い目で手前に折ります。ま
た、空気を抜きます。

Fold the body from the front panel seam back
to the side seam. Smooth out the air.

衽の縫い目
Front panel seam

向こう側の衽を手前に持ってきて、衿同
士、衽同士をぴったりと合わせる。

Bring the front panel on the far side toward
you. Match the collars and front panels
together neatly.

向こう側の衽
Front panel on the far side

127

ゆかたのたたみ方

▶ How To

⑤ 向こう側の脇縫いを手前に持ってきて、脇
縫い同士を合わせます。

Bring the side seam on the far side toward
you. Match the side seams together.

向こう側の脇縫い
Side seam on the far side

⑥ 半分の長さになるぐらいに裾を折って、ゆ
かた全体を右に移動させ、衿側をたたむ
準備をします。

Fold the skirt in half. Move the yukata to the
right. Now you're ready to fold the collar.

➡ 移動 Move

128

衿は衿肩あきの位置を頂点にしてきれい
に三角に折ります。

Fold the collar neatly into a triangle at the
collar shoulder points.

衿肩あき
Collar shoulder points

 衿先まできちんと重ねます。

Match the collar to the ends.

▸ How To

 向こう側の袖を手前に持ってきて重ねます。

Bring the sleeve on the far side over the near sleeve.

 上になっている袖を袖つけ線で折り返します。

Fold the sleeve on top back at the seam.

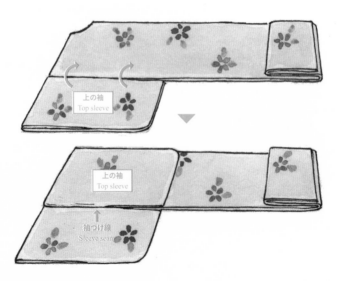

折り上げる裾は肩線の少し手前までにしておきます。重ねてしまうと、部分的な厚みが出て、シワになります。

Fold up to a little below the shoulder line. If they overlap the extra thickness may cause wrinkles.

 衿先の位置で裾を折ります。

Fold the bottom up at the collar ends.

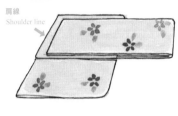

肩線
Shoulder line

 袖つけと振りの位置を両手で持って持ち上げ、残った袖をゆかたの下に折りこみます。

Lift up the yukata at the top and the bottom of the sleeve and fold the sleeve underneath.

振り
Sleeve below the armhole

袖つけ
Sleeve seam

 たたみ上がりです。

Finished.

背や肩線などがきちんとそろっていることが大切です。

Make sure the back and the shoulder line are neatly lined up.

背
Back

肩線
Shoulder line

ゆかたのしまい方

Storing Your Yukata

▸ How To

1

クリーニングに出した場合は、ついてくるビニールや不織布を取ります。

If you took it to a dry cleaner, take it out of the plastic or non-woven fabric bag.

2

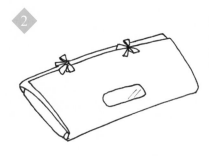

たとう紙、または木綿の大判風呂敷に包んでたんすの中に保管します。

Fold it up in kimono wrapping paper or a large cotton furoshiki for storage.

3

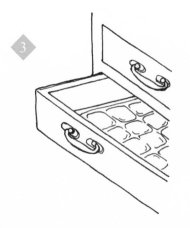

ウール素材は防虫剤が必要ですが、木綿素材のゆかたは必要ありません。むしろ湿気に気をつけましょう。また、ウール素材のものと一緒にしまわないようにします。

Wool needs moth balls, but with cotton you need to be careful about moisture. Do not store together with woolen items.

ゆかたの季節も終わり、きれいに洗濯したら、つぎの夏まできちんと保管しましょう。

After yukata season is over, wash and store it for next summer.

保管するたんすがない場合
If you don't have a chest of drawers

箱や衣装ケースを利用しましょう。ここでは、スーツの箱に入れる例を紹介します。

You can use a box or a plastic clothing case. Here is an example with a box used for a suit.

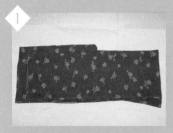

ゆかたをたたみます。

Fold the yukata.

箱の長さに合わせてゆかたを折ります。衿先側から折るようにしましょう。

Fold into the length of the box. Fold from the collar.

木綿の大判風呂敷を箱の上に広げておき、その上にゆかたをのせます。

Lay out a large furoshiki in the box. Place the yukata on top.

風呂敷で包んで、箱のふたをして保管します。

Wrap the yukata in the furoshiki and close the box.

肌着のたたみ方
Folding the Underwear

肌襦袢のたたみ方
Underwear top

1

背中心
Back seam

袖つけ線 Sleeve seam

肌襦袢を広げて、背中心で背中合
わせに折ります。

Spread out and fold the back in half at
the center.

2

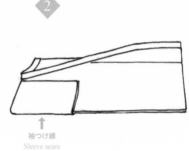

袖つけ線
Sleeve seam

左右の袖を袖つけ線で一緒に上
に折ります。

Fold both sleeves on top at the sleeve
seam.

3

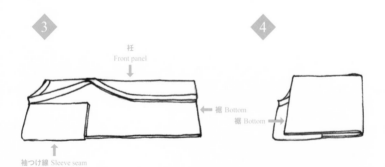

衽
Front panel

裾 Bottom

袖つけ線 Sleeve seam

衽を手前に折ります。

Fold the front panel toward you.

4

裾 Bottom

収納するたんすや引き出しのサイ
ズに合わせて裾を折ります。

Fold the bottom up to fit the size of
the drawer used for storage.

134

1年後にまた気持ちよく着るために、シーズンが終わったらしっかり洗ってアイロンをかけ、きちんとたたみましょう。

Wash, iron and fold up neatly at the end of the season for comfortable wear next year.

ワンピースタイプのたたみ方
Folding one-piece underwear

1

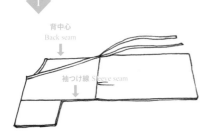

背中心
Back seam

袖つけ線 Sleeve seam

肌着を広げて、背中心で背中合わせにたたみます。

Spread out and fold the back in half at the center.

2

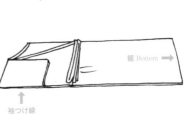

裾 Bottom

袖つけ線
Sleeve seam

左右の袖を2枚重ねたまま、袖つけ線で一緒に折り、紐も2本重ねてきれいに折ります。

Fold both sleeves up at the sleeve seam. Fold the tie strings together neatly.

3

③をひっくり返す
Turn upside down

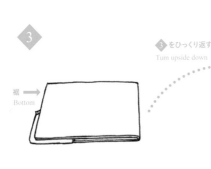

裾
Bottom

裾から折って長さを2分の1にします。

Fold the bottom up in half.

4

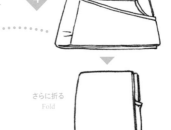

さらに折る
Fold

収納スペースに合わせてさらに折る場合は、ひっくり返してから、サイズに合わせて裾を折ります。

If you need to fold more to fit the space, turn upside down and fold the bottom.

小物のたたみ方・しまい方

Folding and Storing Accessories

帯
Obi

汗や汚れが気になる場合は、クリーニングに出したり、呉服屋さんに相談したりしましょう。汚れが少ないときは、ひと晩干したあと、手のし（手のひらでシワを伸ばす）をします。アイロンはかけなくて大丈夫です。ビニールやたとう紙に入れずにそのまま収納してもよいでしょう。

If the obi shows perspiration marks or other stains you can get it dry cleaned or ask a kimono store what to do. If only slightly dirty, hang it up overnight and then smooth out any wrinkles with your hand. You don't need to iron. If you wish, you can store it unwrapped without putting it inside a plastic bag or kimono wrapping paper.

単の帯
Hitoe obi (single layer)

て先を中にして、裏側が外側になるようにクルクルと巻いていきます。

Bring the tesaki to the center. Roll up with the wrong side of the fabric on the outside.

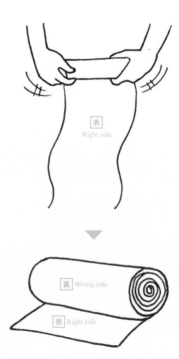

表
Right side

裏 Wrong side

表 Right side

つぎに着るときのことを考えながら、小物もていねいにたたみ、
しまいましょう。

Fold and store neatly for the next time you will use them.

小袋帯（二重に織られた帯）
Kofukuro obi (double layer)

表側が中になるように半分に折り、
また半分に折りを繰り返してたた
んでいきます。

Fold in half with the right side of the
fabric on the inside. Continue folding
by half.

裏 Wrong side

裏 Wrong side

帯揚げ
Obiage cloth

1

シワが多い場合はアイロンをかけ
ます。絹は当て布をして低温で。

Iron out any wrinkles. When ironing
silk, use a low temperature iron and
use a press cloth so the iron does not
directly touch the fabric.

2

半分に折り、また半分に折りを繰
り返し、収納スペースに合う大き
さにたたみます。

Fold in half and continue folding in
half to fit the storage space.

帯締め パターンA
Obijime tie pattern A

四つ折り、または六
つ折りにします。

Fold in fourths or
sixths.

真ん中をセロハン
や紙で留め、このま
ましまいます。

Tie at the middle with
cellophane or paper
and store unwrapped.

帯締め パターンB
Obijime tie pattern B

二つ折りにして蝶
結びにします。

Fold in half and tie in
a bow.

この状態でしまい
ます。

Store unwrapped.

帯締め パターンC
Obijime tie pattern C

二つ折りにして片
結びします。結び目
は上のほうに。

Fold in half and tie a
half knot toward the
top.

クローゼットなどに
下げて収納します。

Hang in your closet.

帯締めのふさがバサバサになっていたら
If the obijime tassels are messy

やかんに湯をわかし、本体をハンカチなどで包んで、ふさを蒸気に当てます。

Boil water in a kettle. Wrap a handkerchief or other cloth around the obijime and hold the tassel in the steam.

水分を含んでふさがきれいに伸びたら、クシや指で整えます。

When the tassels are damp and straight, comb with a comb or your fingers.

セロハンや紙をしっかり巻きつけ、テープで留めます。

Wrap tightly with cellophane or paper and tape.

ふさの端まで巻きを移動させます。

Move the wrapping to the end of the tassel.

ふさが先から飛び出していたら、そのまま巻き紙をスライドさせて、巻き紙ごとハサミで切ってそろえます。ふさの先端が輪になっているものは切らないよう注意しましょう。

If tassel ends stick out, slide the wrapping up and cut through the wrapping to even up the ends. Do NOT cut if the tassels ends are loops.

腰紐 パターンA
Koshihimo pattern A

1

紐先から三角に折りはじめます。このとき三角の頂点が紐の真ん中にくるようにします。

Fold in a triangle starting from one end. Fold to bring the point of the triangle to the center of the sash.

2

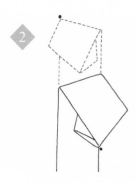

2回折ると五角形になるので、あとは紐の幅に合わせながら折っていきます。

The second fold will make a pentagon. Continue folding matching the width of the sash.

3

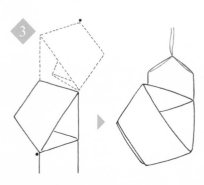

最後は端を内側に折り入れます。

Fold the end inside.

4

コンパクトに収納でき、シワも伸びて、つぎもきれいに使えます。

Folded small with the wrinkles smoothed out, it will be ready to use again.

腰紐 パターンB
Koshihimo pattern B

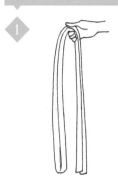

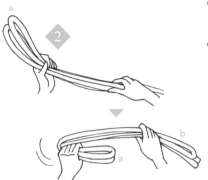

四つ折りにします。

Fold in fourths.

a側にある手首を回転させて、手の甲にbを巻きつけます。

Rotate your wrist on the (a) side and wrap (b) around the back of your hand.

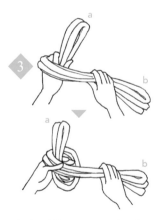

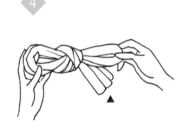

左手を手前に回し、できた輪の中に右手側の紐を入れて、変形の蝶結びにします。

Turn your left hand toward you. Insert the sash in your right hand through the loop made with your left hand. Tie in a lop-sided bow.

使うときは▲の紐をまとめて引っ張るとすぐに解けます。

When you want to use the sash, pull on ▲ and the knot will come loose all at once.

下駄
Geta clogs

水で濡らしてかたく絞った布で、いちばん
汚れている鼻緒のつけ根からかかとまで
の表面をふきます。

Wring the water out of a cloth and wipe the
surface from the dirtiest part, where the thong
attaches, back to the heel.

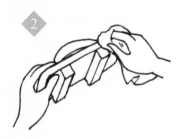

側面をふき、よく乾かしてから紙に包み、
箱の中に入れて保管します。割り箸を箱
の底に入れておくとカビにくくなります。

Wipe the sides. Dry well, wrap in a cloth and
store in a box. Put disposable chopsticks in the
bottom of the box to reduce mold.

Profile
安田多賀子 (やすだ たかこ)

岐阜県生まれ。衣食住の洋風化が進む時代、きものの文化や礼儀作法が継承されていくことを願い、きもの教室をスタート。昭和53 (1978) 年に現在の「装賀きもの学院」を創立。同学院院長として、また小笠原惣領家三十二世直門礼法講師、衣紋道髙倉流たかくら会中部道場会頭、小笠原家茶道古流師範として、国内外を問わず日本の伝統文化の紹介に努めている。(一社) 全日本きもの振興会専任講師、NPO法人和の未来理事長も兼任。

Takako Yasuda

Born in Gifu Prefecture. Yasuda opened her kimono school because she wanted to pass on the traditional culture and manners of kimono now that the Japanese lifestyle is becoming more and more westernized. She established her current school, the Sohga Kimono Institute in 1978. Yasuda is dedicated to helping people in Japan and around the world learn more about traditional Japanese culture.

装賀きもの学院

岐阜県岐阜市真砂町10丁目8番地
TEL 058-263-1250 FAX 058-263-1252
http://www.sohga-g.jp/

協力/Acknowledgements

大下直子 (『和の生活マガジン花saku』編集部)
長谷川功

望月久美子

装賀きもの学院

井登美株式会社
株式会社近喜
三勝株式会社
紫織庵 (丸栄株式会社)
株式会社竹田嘉兵衛商店
株式会社竺仙
株式会社中川染工場
松原伸生
株式会社丸森

協力／井登美

本書は、『和の生活マガジン 花saku』（株式会社PR現代 発行）の連載「目からウロコのきもの塾 安田多賀子のさくら塾」（2008年4月号～2013年3月号）を中心にまとめた当社刊『安田多賀子のゆかた塾』に加筆・修正をし、英語訳をつけて再編集をしたものです。

Staff
撮影/Photo 内田祐介、平野谷雅和、三浦 明、尾﨑たまき
イラスト/Illustration 中西育子
デザイン/Design NILSON（望月昭秀、木村由香利）
編集/Editor 長尾美穂
翻訳/Translator Seacord Laurel

Japanese-English Bilingual Books
How to Wear and Care for Japanese Traditional Summer Attire
The Yukata Handbook

基本からお手入れまで ふだんづかいの楽しみ方
英語訳付き
ゆかたの着つけハンドブック

NDC 593

2015年5月22日　発　行

著　者	安田多賀子
発行者	小川雄一
発行所	株式会社 誠文堂新光社
	〒113-0033
	東京都文京区本郷3-3-11
	（編集）電話03-5805-7285
	（販売）電話03-5800-5780
	http://www.seibundo-shinkosha.net/
印刷所	株式会社 大熊整美堂
製本所	和光堂 株式会社

ISBN978-4-416-71539-0

協力／井登美